POINTS OF INTEREST

POINTS OF INTEREST

A Somewhat Illustrated Collection of Cinquains and Haikus

Andrew McCarter

Belay Press

Cover design and illustrations by Andrew McCarter

CONTENTS

HELLO...

The poems in this book started life as fun standalone ideas that, over time and in hindsight, turned out to be a meandering love letter to my hometown of Jersey. They explore and take inspiration from some of our varied history, interesting places and diverse wildlife. With plenty of random segues thrown in for good measure.

Points of Interest is presented as a kind of unguided tour. A road trip of sorts, with no particular place to go and absolutely no rush to get there. If you are in any way curious where these poems take place or where the inspiration came from. The map on the following page may help... but probably not, as it is somewhat vague and questionably accurate.

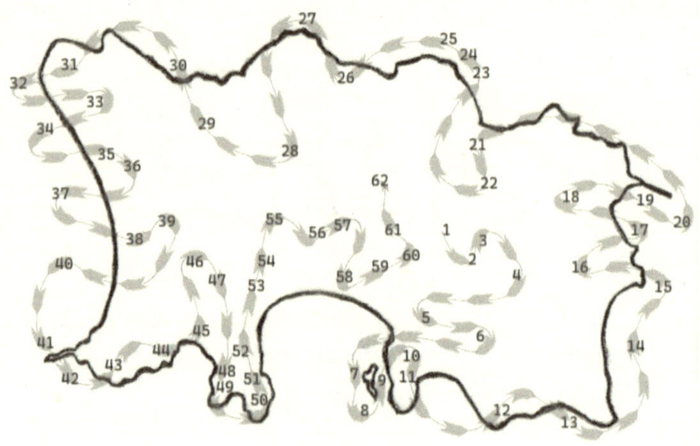

As promised a somewhat vague and
questionably accurate map.

POEMS...

Sunshine Isle

Jersey
Golden sunshine
Yellow sands meet warm sea
Happy smiles on sunburnt faces
Summer

blue waves, peaceful breeze
sunshine bright on sandy shores
pleasant summer day

Cow #1

Ode to
Bovine beauty
Legacy of Jersey
A breed of heritage and charm
Daisy

lesson from a cow
appreciate here and now
learn how to be still

Cow #2

Daily
They cross the road
A country traffic jam
Calmly following the farmer
Fresh milk

between two green fields
trooping across the tarmac
promise of fresh grass

La Hougue Bie

Neolithic #1

Sunrise

Supplication

Daily resurrection

Spiritual awakening

Sacred

memories in stone

rituals of life and death

builders' ghosts remain

Pub Dog

Pub dog
Ever watchful
Seeker of fallen crisps
A benevolently played game
Good boy

the regulars pause
relief from their daily grind
scratch behind the ear

Used To Be A Wolf

Wild wolf
Your ancient kin
Primal roots long buried
Shelter and comfort at a cost
Now tamed

used to be a wolf
now with squeaky toy held tight
belly rubs hold sway

Castle #1

Granite

Cold-weathered stone

Defiant Sentinel

Strong defence against invaders

Fortress

once the tide recedes

no longer cut off from shore

a lifeline revealed

Ghost

Shadow
Lingering still
Ethereal figure
Unfinished business to resolve
Haunted

echoes of the lost
footsteps on the empty stairs
the past does not rest

St Helier's Hermitage

Hermitage

Alone
Seeking solace
Peaceful sanctuary
Refuge found in contemplation
Simple

hermit's solitude
Helier's meditation
faith against the dark

Steam Clock

Worn out
No tick, no tock
Rusted gears, broken cogs
empty hands mark time twice a day
Silent

steam clock stands broken
monument to time, frozen
engineer needed

Smokestack

Rubbish
Turned to green fuel
Tall chimney fills the sky
Pollutants filtered, now clean air
Renewed

energy from waste
new resources from old garbage
earth breathes easier

Cloud Watching

Drifting
Inspiration
across the blue canvas
Imagination is set free
Day dream

white shapes drifting by
a beautiful silent show
subconscious runs wild

Stars (Hope)

We are
Made of stardust
Forged in Supernova
Home to infinite mysteries
Wonder

◆ ◆ ◆

distant diamonds shine
dreams shared with the great beyond
stars make no reply

Moon/Tides

Witness
The ebb and flow
Every ripple and wave
Alluring celestial pull
Lovers

moonlight on the waves
tide drawn to her silver charm
timeless seduction

Castle #2

Guarding
Jersey's sunrise
Ramparts salute the dawn
Grey granite streaked with golden light
Glory

medieval walls
bustling harbours protector
weight of history

La Pouquelaye De Faldouet

AMc

Neolithic #2

Old bones
Burial grounds
Necklaces and arrows
A tribute, history enshrined
Remains

sombre ring of stones
secrets linger in the air
dark shadows lengthen

Beach #1

Spiral
Recurring form
A unique work of art
Fractal curves mirror galaxies
Sublime

seashells flowing curves
holding echo's of the waves
treasures from the deep

In The Pines #1

Shifting
Accidental
Fragmented shadows cast
The forest floor, nature's canvas
Patterns

sunlight through needles
dappled shadows in the pines
nature's mosaic

Breakwater

The dream
Half built, yet strong
Waves crash to no avail
A testament to endurance
Steadfast

strolling hand in hand
the distant horizon calls
greeting the sunrise

Dolphin

Hopeful
It's a big sea
Scanning the horizon
Elusive dolphin, wild and free
Leaping

◆ ◆ ◆

ocean's poetry
written in a playful leap
spirit of the sea

The Black Dog

Black Dog

Legend
A chilling howl
Eyes as big as saucers
Stalking fear across shadowed cliffs
Black Dog

haunting Bouley Bay
stories whispered after dark
warning of lost love

The Zoo

The Zoo
Concrete Jungle
Holding captive beauty
The high cost of conservation
Worth it

freedom behind bars
endangered species' last hope
complex emotions

Wolf's Lair #1

Wolf's Lair
Now abandoned
Guarding against attack
Napoleonic protection
History

mindful solitude
self-reliance, simple life
transcendental peace

Wolf's Lair #2

Simple
Weathered cottage
Fire glows, contentment found
Alone with thoughts and inner peace
Idyll

cabin in the woods
self-sufficiency calling
reflecting on life

Wolf's Lair #3

Landing
Allied forces
Operation Hardtack
Christmas day nineteen forty-four
Courage

danger treads unseen
silent boots, through shadows creep
the night holds its breath

Up

Heavy
Rhythmic footsteps
Muscles loudly protest
Life-affirming accomplishment
Summit

muscles burn, heart pounds
each step a victory won
pause, enjoy the view

Lighthouse #1

Beacon
Light the darkness
Standing against the night
Lost sailors safely guided home
Comfort

incandescent hope
lighthouse watches through the night
you are not alone

Shadow Flower

Flower (Shadow)

Hidden
Secret garden
Luminous beauty thrives
Moonbeams revealing unseen blooms
Sublime

unseen by the sun
moonlight reveals it's form
shadow flower glows

In The Pines #2

Beneath
A tangled web
Where shadows twist and dance
Hidden secrets, best left buried
Old woods

ancient woods whisper
nature's wild heart beats unheard
find peace in silence

Breakie

Sizzle
Pure and simple
Culinary delight
Weekend temptation satisfied
Fry up

◆ ◆ ◆

local greasy spoon
the hungover pilgrimage
bacon rolls allure

Grosnez Castle

Castle #3

Moss-grown
Weathered archway
Stark against the sunset
A silent witness to day's end
Stoic

a castle of old
weather-worn ancient stronghold
relic of the past

Stars (Perihelion)

Orbit
A complex waltz
Gravitational pull
Grand celestial mechanics
Return

gravity's embrace
sun's bright heart, a fiery kiss
earth's orbital dance

Walkies

Daily
Shared ritual
Bounding out the front door
Every walk a new adventure
Faithful

he goes nose to ground
through the grass, joyful tail wags
man's best friend indeed

The Pinnacle

The Pinnacle

Advice
Think with your feet
Pull harder, strength tested
Don’t let go, and you won’t fall off
Maybe…

weathered sentinel
guarding Jersey’s rugged coast
lonely seagull cries

Potato #1

Patience
A season's work
Nature's bounty revealed
New potatoes freshly unearthed
Reward

green leaves standing tall
promise held beneath the ground
harvest begins soon

Potato #2

Boiled
A simple dish
Chopped mint and pinch of salt
Generous helping of butter
Tasty

the Jersey Royal
treasure gathered from the earth
culinary treat

Beach #2

Breathing
Fully present
Worries begin to fade
Footprints washed away with the tide
Tranquil

barefoot on the sand
every step a conscious choice
finding mindfulness

White House

Refuge
Le Don Hilton
This little white cottage
Still standing strong against the storm
Shelter

◆ ◆ ◆

a simple dwelling
whitewashed walls and humble charm
somewhere to unwind

Duck

Yellow
Tiny fluff ball
Exploring the green pond
Safe under mother's watchful gaze
Learning

on top all is calm
underneath frantic paddling
reflection of life

Surf's Up

Riding
Azure contours
Irresistible line
The edge of chaos and control
Balance

counting rhythmic swells
waiting for the perfect break
patience rewarded

Corbière Lighthouse

Lighthouse #2

High tide
Enveloping
Ocean claims the causeway
Concrete lifeline, isolated
Patience

dark clouds gathering
guiding light cuts through the storm
ships safe passage home

Beach #3

Sprinkles
Vanilla cone
Summer's simple pleasure
Sweet indulgence, melting too fast
Classic

seagulls circle high
hoping for a dropped ice-cream
scavenger's patrol

Green Lizard

Gleaming
Emerald lizard
Master of camouflage
A tiny wonder rarely seen
Vanished

miniature dragon
echoes from the days of yore
soaking up the sun

Owl #1

Hunter
Heightened senses
Soundless aviator
Gliding through the darkening woods
Nocturne

soft feathers, sharp eyes
phantom flies on silent wings
shadow hunts tonight

Owl #2

Trembling
Sensing danger
No hiding place in sight
Desperate eyes reflect the moonlight
Done for

shrouded in long grass
unaware and unhidden
circled from above

Red Squirrel

Darting
Red in the trees
Bushy-tailed woodland friend
Quick and agile hoarder of nuts
Instinct

leaping, auburn blur
gravity defied once more
unafraid dancer

Hedgehog

Alert
Treading softly
A tiny warrior
Wears a coat of spiky armour
Hunter

hedgerow wanderer
living, breathing pincushion
lone nocturnal knight

Mammoths

Mammoths
Great shaggy herd
Against the ice and snow
Across the land through blizzards cruel
Roaming

hairy elephants
walked the earth in times long past
only bones remain

Hunters

Sharing
Campfire stories
Across the dancing flames
Sheltered from the ravaging cold
Family

chased towards the cliffs
hunters' spears fly sharp and true
mammoth’s doom is near

Noirmont Guns

Silent Guns

Symbol
Of battles past
Of sacrifice and pain
Of courage, honour, peace and hope
Homage

memories of war
rusting anti-aircraft guns
now a perch for birds

Little Brown Birds

Humble
Melodic song
Flitting through the hedgerows
A faithful friend in every park
Noble

little brown jobbies
Sparrow, Dunnock, Chiffchaff, Wren
nondescript beauty

In The Pines #3

She runs
Down the worn path
Marathon in four weeks
Footfalls steady, breathing controlled
Prepared

silent barren pines
ancient trees and hidden trails
nature's place to breathe

Occupation #1

Stolen
Idyllic life
Now uncertain future
Island's freedom oppressed with fear
Endure

jackboots on our soil
dark times for this sunny isle
occupation dawns

Occupation #2

Secret
Radios bring
News from across the sea
Fuelling clandestine flames of hope
Resist

◆ ◆ ◆

quiet defiance
painted “V” for victory
island’s strength remains

Determination

AMc

Flower (Determination)

Growing
The hairline crack
Small green leaf emerges
A fragile sign of nature's strength
New life

new leaf unfurling
daisy bursting through the cracks
determination

Liberation #1

At last

Allies triumph

Victory in Europe

Red Cross ship "The Beagle" brings peace

Three cheers

liberation comes

occupied for five hard years

Union Flags fly proud

Liberation #2

Old scars
Speak of hard times
Healed wounds and lives rebuilt
Reconciling past and future
Forgive

silent reflection
for those who were lost, unseen
sacrificed for us

Ville-Ès-Nouaux

Neolithic #3

Circles
Fading with time
Calendar of the past
Reminder of what was once known
Echoes

◆ ◆ ◆

built before the cross
neolithic enigma
buried in the past

Old Friends

Old friends
Shared history
Reliving memories
Putting the world to rights once more
Grateful

bald and grey-haired now
wrinkles deepen year by year
laughs remain the same

Pub

Local
Simple pleasures
Golden liquid sunshine
Afternoon blends into the night
Who's round?

a pint shared with friends
beer garden, sanctuary
respite from life's woes

Hangover

I swear
"Never again!"
The traditional lie
Strong coffee and fry-up required
Get up!

head pounds, stomach churns
the ninth pint was a mistake
deep regret sets in

Home

Built on
Strong foundations
More than bricks and mortar
Promising comfort, love and peace
Welcome

safe and understood
acceptance without judgement
home is not a place

A FEW NOTES

Pub Dog, Used to be a Wolf and Walkies - These six poems form what I pretentiously, with tongue firmly in cheek, call my Doggo Trilogy. They are dedicated to three very good boys. Tux, Parker and Tate.

Ghost - I've no idea if Elizabeth Castle has a ghost or not. But I got the idea for these two poems while I was there, so maybe...?

Potato #1 & #2 - Dedicated with respect to Samwise Gamgee

The Pinnacle - I used to be a climber, before I broke myself once too often. This cinquain sums up useful climbing skills I learnt but didn't always put into practice.

Wolf's Lair #3, Silent Guns, Occupation #1 & #2 and Liberation #1 & #2 - were all written on May 9th, which is Jersey's Liberation Day. Clearly I was feeling particularly patriotic.

Old Friends, Pub, Hangover - The unholy trinity of good times.

CHEERS

Thank you for reading my poems.
I hope you enjoyed them.

If you have any thoughts, comments or feedback, please feel free to get in touch via belaypress@gmail.com

www.ingramcontent.com/pod-product-compliance
Lightning Source LLC
LaVergne TN
LVHW051016080826
845145LV00009B/2662

* 9 7 8 1 9 1 9 5 6 0 5 0 2 *